I Am George Lucas

By Grace Norwich

Illustrated by
Elisabeth Alba

SCHOLASTIC INC.

Contents

Introduction

I've been called the force behind the Force.

In 1977, my movie *Star Wars*, with its immortal line, "May the Force be with you," opened in a few dozen movie theaters around the country. Science fiction wasn't all that popular back then, so expectations were pretty low for my story, set "a long time ago in a galaxy far, far away. . . ." Plus, I wasn't exactly a household name in the 1970s, even though I'd already written and directed a few other films.

To be honest, I wasn't sure *Star Wars* would cause much of a splash, either. Not that I didn't believe in the movie. It's just that *Star Wars* was so incredibly different from anything that had come before it. I didn't know if audiences would get it.

I still remember the day the movie premiered. It was May 25, 1977, and my wife and I were driving to dinner at the Hamburger Hamlet, a popular restaurant in Hollywood, California. I was wiped out from weeks of film editing and was looking forward to going to Hawaii the next day for some much needed relaxation.

All of a sudden, the traffic on Hollywood Boulevard came to a stop. I couldn't figure out what was going on. But then I saw it: masses of people making their way to the Chinese Theatre, a popular movie theater across the street from the hamburger place. I looked up and saw what was playing: *Star Wars*. As we sat in the restaurant, we watched in wonder as fans streamed into the theater.

Over the coming weeks and months, audiences continued visiting theaters all over the country to enter the incredible world that I'd created for them. Many of these fans would

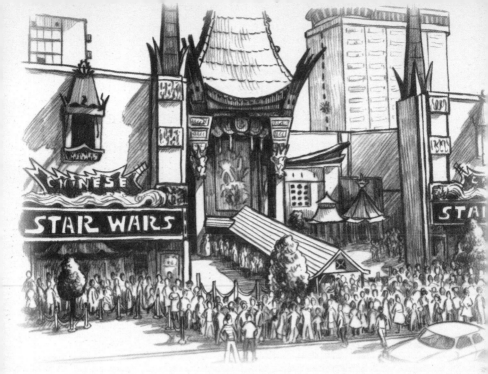

see the movie again and again. In fact, there are stories of people paying to see *Star Wars* hundreds of times!

In its first weekend, playing in a limited number of theaters, the movie made about $1.5 million. When it opened "wide" in hundreds of other theaters, it raked in just under $7 million in its first weekend. In the end, *Star Wars* would earn $775 million worldwide, making it one of the highest-grossing films of all time.

But *Star Wars* was just the beginning. As you're about to learn, the movie that turned me into a true Hollywood legend practically overnight was just the first in a series of projects that would change the way we think about movies.

And the Force was with me all along. I am George Lucas.

People You Will Meet

GEORGE LUCAS:
Hollywood legend and creator of some of the most popular movie series of all time.

GEORGE LUCAS, SR.:
George's father, a successful businessman from Modesto, California.

WENDY LUCAS:
George's younger sister, with whom he was closest growing up.

STEVEN SPIELBERG:
Hollywood director who worked with George on the Indiana Jones films.

HARRISON FORD:
One of George's go—to actors, he played a lead in the *Star Wars* and Indiana Jones franchises.

MARK HAMILL:
The TV actor who played Luke Skywalker in the *Star Wars* films.

CARRIE FISHER:
The actress who played Princess Leia in the *Star Wars* films.

MARCIA GRIFFIN:
George's first wife, whom he married in 1969.

FRANCIS FORD COPPOLA:
Hollywood director who acted as George's mentor during his early caree

Time Line

May 14, 1944

George Walton Lucas, Jr., is born in Modesto, California.

June 12, 1962

A terrible car accident nearly claims George's life.

1971

THX 1138, George's first feature film, is released.

1973

George has his first major success with the release of *American Graffiti*.

May 21, 1980

The Empire Strikes Back is released, and Lucas creates Skywalker Sound.

June 14, 1981

Raiders of the Lost Ark is released, with Lucas as co-executive producer.

May 19, 1999

The Phantom Menace is released.

May 19, 2002

Attack of the Clones is released.

1966	1969
George graduates from the University of Southern California film school.	George marries Marcia Griffin.

May 25, 1977	1978
Star Wars is released, winning seven Academy Awards and, to date, making $775 million.	George purchases property in Marin County, California, for what will become Skywalker Ranch.

May 25, 1983	1987
Return of the Jedi is released, completing the *Star Wars* trilogy.	George establishes LucasArts Learning.

May 19, 2005	2012
Revenge of the Sith is released.	Disney acquires Lucasfilm Ltd. for $4 billion.

CHAPTER ONE

Modesto Beginnings

If Los Angeles, California, is the most glamorous place in the country, full of movie stars, fancy cars, and luxury homes, the city of Modesto is just the opposite. Located in the central valley of Northern California, roughly ninety miles east of San Francisco, it's a sleepy destination surrounded by sprawling farmland and not much else.

As quiet as Modesto is today, back in the

1930s, it was even quieter. Less than fifteen thousand people lived there at the time, which gave the city a small-town feel. You couldn't walk down Main Street without bumping into someone you knew. And chances are that particular someone would be having a hard time making ends meet.

That's because in the 1930s, the nation was in the middle of the Great Depression, a severe

economic crisis that affected much of the world. Lots of folks were out of work and many families were losing their homes, including in Modesto.

It was not the ideal time or the place to be starting a family. But George Walton Lucas, Sr., was not the type of man who let outside forces get in his way. Indeed, at a time when many people were losing their jobs, he managed to not only find work with a stationery store in downtown Modesto, but also to become a part owner of the business.

George Sr. had also done well by marrying Dorothy Bomberger, the beautiful daughter of a prominent local family. The pair met in high school. It was love at first sight for George Sr., who went home and told his mother that he'd met the girl he was going to marry. Sure enough, they were married in 1933, when George Sr. was twenty and Dorothy just eighteen. A year later, the young couple had their first child, a daughter named Ann. A second daughter, Katherine, was born two years later.

These were happy times for the Lucas family. George Sr. continued to thrive in his business and they were able to move into a newly built home. Maybe the only thing missing was a son. Unfortunately, Dorothy's health was failing, so her doctors discouraged her from having more children. But somewhat miraculously, she became pregnant again. On Sunday, May 14, 1944, she gave birth to a five-pound, fourteen-ounce baby boy with his father's dark eyes and pointy ears. Given the strong **resemblance**, they decided to call him George Walton Lucas, Jr.

George's early years were filled with love from two caring big sisters and his adoring mom and dad. There was also a kind and caring housekeeper named Till who ran the household when Dorothy's illness became too serious.

George would even be blessed with a younger

sibling of his own, a sister named Wendy who was born three years after him. The two youngest Lucas children were inseparable as kids, and their closeness continued all the way into adulthood.

From an early age, George had **boundless** energy and an active imagination. Together with his boyhood pals John Plummer and George Frankenstein he would often create elaborate rides and events in the backyard. One

day the boys even made a zoo, using various neighborhood pets as the animals.

George nourished his imagination with **avid** reading. "I liked all the normal kinds of adventure books, *Kidnapped, Treasure Island, Huck Finn* sorts of things," he once said in an interview. "I loved *Swiss Family Robinson* and that whole period of South Sea adventure movies. I liked Westerns."

As much as George enjoyed reading, it was nothing compared to his love of television, which was just becoming popular in the 1950s. In 1954, George Sr. finally bought the family a black-and-white TV set. They put it on a revolving stand so that young George could watch it from the living room or kitchen. That way he wouldn't miss any of his favorite shows, like Westerns such as *Gunsmoke* and *Maverick* and adventure series like *Flash Gordon Conquers the Universe.*

Now That's a Comic Book Collection!

Comic books were a constant in young George's life. *Batman, Superman, Scrooge McDuck*—you name it, George read it. In fact, George and Wendy used to combine their allowances so that they could buy more comics— more than five hundred in all!

"We had so many that eventually my dad built a big shed in the back, and there was one room strictly devoted to comics, floor to ceiling," Wendy recalled.

All in all, George enjoyed a happy early childhood, one that filled his mind with adventure. As he entered his teenage years, however, he would search for real action and excitement—with near tragic results.

CHAPTER
TWO

A Need for Speed

Throughout most of George's early life, cartoons and television were enough to keep him entertained. But by the time he entered Thomas Downey High School he was ready for something more. Unfortunately, school itself was not going to provide the necessary distraction. Though George did okay in some classes, including art and music, he was basically a C student at best. "One of the big problems I had . . . was that I always wanted to learn something other than what I was being taught," he said.

George's lack of interest in school caused plenty of trouble at home. Though George Sr. was a loving father, he expected a lot from his children, including good grades. But most weekday afternoons, when George Jr. should have been doing his homework, he was instead listening to rock-and-roll music, including Elvis Presley and Chuck Berry, while snacking on Hershey bars and slurping down Coca-Colas.

Rock music and junk food may not help earn straight As in high school, but as bad habits go, they're not exactly life threatening. As George settled into high school, however, he discovered a potentially more dangerous pastime: racing cars.

From an early age, George liked to fix things. "I've always been very into building things," he said, recalling chess sets carved from wood and other handmade creations. Once George discovered cars, he focused all that creative energy on automobiles. "My teenage years . . . were completely devoted to cars," he explained. "That was the most important thing in my life from about the ages of fourteen to twenty."

In the middle of the twentieth century, as cars became a common part of U.S. culture, cruising emerged as a favorite social activity of teenagers all over the country. Cruising was the name for when kids piled in their cars and drove throughout town, while listening to music and looking for other kids to hang out with.

With its wide, flat avenues and popular drive-in hamburger joint, Modesto turned into a major cruising town. Even teens from other towns would drive into Modesto to cruise along its main strip. George found the entire scene totally irresistible. Not only did cruising the streets of Modesto satisfy his love of loud music and hanging out with friends, it also satisfied his obsession with cars.

George didn't love just any old car. It had to be fast. His first car was a Fiat Bianchina bought by his father. It was a nice car, but according to George, "it had a sewing machine motor," meaning it was just too slow. So he spent every day at the local mechanic shop, fixing up the engine until it could easily hit seventy miles per hour.

Unfortunately, with its beefed-up engine, it

wasn't long before George rolled the tiny Fiat during a dangerous accident, flipping the car over and bashing in the roof. Rather than drive more cautiously, he simply cut off the roof and installed a roll bar, turning the Fiat into a speedy little racing car.

As George's passion for cars intensified, he started to look the part of a true "greaser." He wore faded jeans and dingy T-shirts and slicked back his long hair with Vaseline. He also started competing in car races all over the

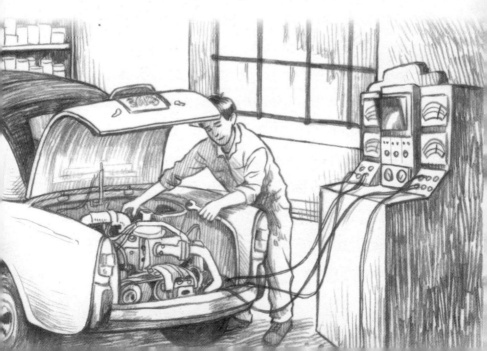

state, earning a reputation as a daring speed demon. Meanwhile, his grades continued to slip throughout his senior year, and there was a chance he would not graduate.

That thought must have been weighing heavily on George's mind on the morning of June 12, 1962. The school year was ending in a few days, and George still had three term papers due, plus final exams. He had no choice but to hit the library.

His sister Wendy, who often helped her big brother with his studies, nearly joined him, but decided to stay at home. George hopped into his Fiat and sped off to the library. He managed to hit the books for a few hours before deciding to head home. And he nearly made it, too. But a short distance from the thirteen-acre walnut farm where the Lucas family lived, a speeding Chevy Impala plowed into the little Fiat, causing it to flip five times before slamming into a walnut tree.

It was not the kind of accident people survive. And when George was first brought in to the hospital, it didn't look good. His heartbeat was quiet, and he was coughing up blood. Miraculously, he pulled through. When he finally woke up, he had no recollection of the accident.

As George lay in his hospital bed, the magnitude of his brush with death hit him. "I realized that I'd been living my life so close to the edge for so long," he said. "That's when I decided to go straight, to be a better student, to try to do something with myself."

CHAPTER
THREE

Time to
Buckle Down

George's near-death experience gave him a new outlook on life. But it didn't change the mediocre grades he'd received throughout high school. Attending a four-year college would be out of the question. Fortunately, his grades were good enough to get George into Modesto Junior College. He decided to go for it.

With the same devotion he'd once saved for cars and racing, George now applied to his classwork at Modesto. His high-school teachers probably wouldn't have recognized the **studious** young man who walked eagerly from sociology class to anthropology to literature to creative writing.

Though George continued to work on cars, his focus was now on academics, and he was pulling in the good grades to prove it. On June 9, 1964, nearly two years to the day from his horrific car crash, George graduated from Modesto Junior College with an associate arts degree.

Now what? George must have thought. He'd always been interested in photography, especially after his father bought him a 35-millimeter camera. At one point, he'd even converted a spare bedroom back home into a darkroom. And more recently, he'd also been experimenting with a friend's 8-millimeter movie camera.

With these ideas bouncing around his mind, he met with his old childhood friend John Plummer, who suggested that George apply to the University of Southern California (USC) in Los Angeles. Around the same time, George was helping build a race car for an established Hollywood cinematographer, who encouraged him to consider USC's film school. Once again, George decided to go for it.

The decision didn't sit well with George Sr. Film school is a popular pursuit these days, but in the 1960s, it was a new field of academic study. If you wanted to work in movies, you basically had to know someone in the industry. No one went to school to become a filmmaker.

George and his father had one of their more heated disagreements. At some point during the argument, maybe after George Sr. begged his son once more to come home and take over the family business, George said to his father, "I'll never be back, and as a matter of fact, I'll be a millionaire before I'm thirty."

From his very first day on campus at USC, George was a man on a mission. While other students goofed off and skipped class, George spent every waking minute mastering the basics of filmmaking, from operating the camera to recording sound. When he wasn't learning about film, he was going to the cinema to watch them, sometimes seeing five films in a single weekend. According to George, this was "a time when I really blossomed. When I went in there, I didn't

The Film School Generation

Prior to the 1960s, most Hollywood directors got into the business through family connections. George was part of a new breed of directors who went to film school and valued the art of filmmaking. Here are a few other members of what's been called the Film School or New Hollywood Generation.

 **Francis Ford Coppola**

Born: April 7, 1939

School: University of California, Los Angeles (UCLA)

Popular Films: *The Godfather* (1972), *Apocalypse Now* (1979), *The Outsiders* (1983)

Brian De Palma

Born: September 11, 1940

School: Columbia University

Popular Films: *Carrie* (1976), *Scarface* (1983), *The Untouchables* (1987)

Martin Scorsese

Born: November 17, 1942

School: New York University (NYU)

Popular Films: *Taxi Driver* (1976), *Goodfellas* (1990), *Gangs of New York* (2002)

Steven Spielberg

Born: December 18, 1946

School: California State University, Long Beach

Popular Films: *Jaws* (1975), *Jurassic Park* (1993), *Saving Private Ryan* (1998)

know anything. The school helped me focus on film, and I loved doing that. They helped me become what I am today."

George also learned what it takes to get a film made. It's one thing to be able to operate a camera, but another to manage a complicated film production. Many of his peers didn't complete a single movie. Not George though. "I made lots of movies while in school while everybody else was running around saying, 'Oh, I wish I could make a movie. I wish they'd give me some film.'"

And the student films George made were very good. He was exceptional at piecing together the various aspects of sound and special effects. His reputation was starting to spread. "George Lucas was always the star of the student festivals then," said his peer Steven Spielberg, who would go on to become an extremely famous Hollywood director.

George was fortunate to have entered film school at a time when the movie industry was changing. His father was right: Hollywood had once been a place where you had to know someone to get ahead. But the industry was starting to embrace the idea of the hot, young cinema students. The only question was: Would George get the chance to shine outside of the student film festivals?

Life in the Real World

George graduated from USC in 1966 with a Bachelor of Arts in cinema and a reputation as one of the most promising young filmmakers in the country. But that didn't mean Hollywood was knocking down his door with offers.

Even if they had, George might have said no. As much as he loved movies, George wasn't crazy about the industry that produced them. Like many up-and-coming directors of the

42

day, he felt that Hollywood put too many limits on creativity.

But George wasn't about to give up on his dream of making movies. And he still had to pay the bills. So he took a job as an assistant working for the United States government on educational and propaganda films geared toward the military.

The Vietnam War was raging in the 1960s. In fact, George was nearly drafted into the war, but during his physical he learned that he had diabetes, a disease caused by high levels of sugar in the blood. The news was upsetting for George, but at least it kept him out of the dangerous jungles of Southeast Asia, where the war was being fought.

Working on government films wasn't the most exciting job. But there was one major attraction for George: a beautiful assistant editor on the project named Marcia Griffin, who also happened to have been born in the same town of Modesto where George grew up. Despite George's shyness, he finally worked up the courage to ask Marcia out on a date. They hit it off and went on more dates, usually to the movies, and before long they were an official couple.

Once George's work for the government ended, he had to decide what to do next. Though he still wasn't crazy about the thought of Hollywood, he decided to accept a scholarship to direct a short film about the making of a Hollywood-produced Western. "I didn't really have much feeling about [Hollywood]," he said. "I thought I'd see for myself and know why I disliked it, rather than just saying it out of hand."

He followed up that scholarship with another from Warner Bros. in 1967. The move would prove life changing, since it put George in close contact with another promising young filmmaker named Francis Ford Coppola.

George's assignment was to learn from Francis as he directed a musical called *Finian's Rainbow*. Francis was five years older than George, and established in his career, but he saw in George a **kindred** spirit whom he could learn from as well. "I was very grateful to have someone of my own generation around to discuss what I was trying to do as opposed to what I was able to do," Francis later recalled. "I very quickly became aware of his superior intelligence."

Though George and Francis had a mutual respect for each other, their personalities were polar opposites, or "like two halves of a whole," as George once put it. Where Francis was loud and brash, George was shy and cautious. Francis lived to be the center of attention, while George preferred the sidelines.

Despite their differences, the two directors

joined forces and started a film company in 1969, the same year that George and Marcia decided to tie the knot. They called the company American Zoetrope (*zoetrope* means "movement of life," and is also the name of a very early form of moving pictures) and opened it in San Francisco, California, far away from the oppressive atmosphere of Hollywood.

Zoetrope might have been far removed from Hollywood, but George and Francis still relied on studio money to get their company off the ground. In his role as president, Francis pitched seven projects to Warner Bros. One of them was *THX 1138*, a futuristic story based on a student film short that George had completed at USC.

Warner Bros. accepted five of the projects,

including *THX 1138*. Just three years out of college, George was given his first shot at a feature-length film, though he was paid only $15,000 to write a script and given a ten-week shooting schedule. Not that George was complaining. "I realized that I might never have the chance again to make this totally off-the-wall movie, without any real supervision," he said.

George shot and edited the film and delivered it to Warner Bros. Unfortunately, the studio executives thought it was too strange.

Film Notes
THX 1138 (1971)

George's job: Co-writer and Director

What's it about?

Set in the distant future, this science-
fiction story features a society underneath
the surface of the earth where people
are controlled by drugs that eliminate
their ability to feel any kind of emotion.
Faceless androids monitor their every
move. But two of the brainwashed
occupants are able to stop taking drugs
and fall in love. They plot their escape
from the underground city to the surface
of the earth, where they can live freely.

Main stars:

Robert Duvall as THX

Donald Pleasence as SEN

Maggie McOmie as LUH

The back-and-forth grew more heated. Not only did the studio demand its money back on this film, it threatened to terminate every deal with Zoetrope.

This was a very dark time in George's life. In the end, Warner Bros. gave in, though their editors ended up cutting about four minutes from *THX 1138*, which made George very angry. The movie came out in 1971 to mixed reviews.

As for American Zoetrope, the setback was too great for the already struggling company. George and Francis were forced to go their separate ways, though their relationship, often based on a friendly rivalry, would continue for many years.

CHAPTER FIVE

Creating an American Classic

Following the failure of *THX 1138*, George did a lot of soul-searching. To this day, his first feature film remains one of his favorites. But he realized that it was very offbeat and unusual. And he worried that his reputation was now that of "a cold, weird director, a science-fiction sort of guy who carried a calculator. And I'm not like that at all. So, I thought, maybe I'll do something exactly the opposite."

That left the question: What's the exact opposite of a futuristic society filled with creepy androids and brainwashed citizens? The answer George came up with was *American Graffiti*, a classic coming-of-age tale set in early 1960s America about four teenage friends celebrating the last night of summer.

The idea for the movie came out of George's own experiences as a teenager. "It all happened to me, but I sort of **glamorized** it," he said in an interview, recalling nights spent cruising the main drag in Modesto, hanging out with friends at the local drive-in.

Rock-and-roll music was a huge part of 1960s American culture, with bands like the Beatles and the Beach Boys filling the airwaves. So George chose to frame the story with songs. "It had music all the way through it," he explained. "Not just the score but actual songs from the period, and that is something that nobody had done before."

Unfortunately, the major studios were scared off by all the music, since getting the rights to use songs in a movie can be expensive. George also had a hard time lining up the best writers to help polish up his script.

The challenges of moviemaking were really starting to bother George. In fact, there were times when he thought about giving up altogether. "My first six years in the business were hopeless," he recalls. "There's lot of times when you sit and you say, 'Why am I doing this? I'll never make it. It's just not going to happen.

I should really go out and get a real job, and try to survive.'"

But as George would learn, success in Hollywood is all about **perseverance**. Anyone can come up with an idea for a movie. But it's the rare individual who has the ability to translate that vision onto the big screen.

So George continued to push for *American Graffiti*. Finally, Universal Studios agreed to take a chance on the film—though they gave George only $600,000 and a shooting schedule of just twenty-eight days.

In order to meet the budget, George had to cut the number of songs from eighty to about forty-five. But he was firm in his desire to cast the film with fresh faces, rather than established stars. Ron Howard, Richard Dreyfuss, and Harrison Ford were among the relative unknowns picked by George who would go on to have huge careers.

George was off to a relatively good start. But

once shooting began, he was reminded again of how hard it is to get a movie made. First, the town in California where the film was supposed to be shot backed out of the deal. Also, the film had to be shot entirely at night, as that's when the story takes place. This presented technical challenges, especially with the lighting. It was also hard for George, an early-to-bed, early-to-rise kind of guy, to make the adjustment.

After a grueling month, the shoot was finally finished. George was ready to preview it for the studio. As with *THX 1138*, the response

Film Notes
American Graffiti (1973)

George's job: Co-writer and Director

What's it about?

Set in the 1960s, this coming-of-age story follows a group of teenagers on the last night of summer. Two of the characters, Curt and Steve, are supposed to leave for college the next morning, but both have their doubts about going. The teens spend the night cruising around in their cars and having an all-around wild time. In the morning, the friends go their separate ways, where they'll come to different ends.

Main stars:

Richard Dreyfuss as Curt

Ron Howard as Steve

Paul Le Mat as John

Charles Martin Smith as Terry

Harrison Ford as Bob Falfa

was mixed. Fortunately, the film had plenty of supporters, including Francis Ford Coppola, who offered to buy *American Graffiti* from Universal if they refused to take it.

In the end, Universal came around, though they insisted on cutting about four and a half minutes of footage, which drove George crazy. "I was really angry, and I remain angry to this day," he said. That's when he vowed never to give up control of a movie again.

Despite those bad feelings, *American Graffiti* had a very happy ending. When it finally opened on August 1, 1973, lines snaked around the block. And as word of the movie spread, audiences flocked to see it. A film that cost a total of $777,000 to produce would eventually earn the studio $115 million. And it would be nominated for five Academy Awards, including Best Director and Best Original Screenplay for George.

Less than a decade had passed since George swore to his father that he would be a millionaire before the age of thirty. As his profit share of *American Graffiti* rolled in, totaling more than $7 million, it was clear that the twenty-nine-year-old George had more than lived up to his word.

Star Wars Is Born

Success can do strange things to a person, especially in Hollywood. George had seen it before, with once-decent filmmakers becoming lazy and **corrupt** by power and money. He explains, "Here you've spent your whole life just begging, and using every means at your disposal to get one person or two people to say 'yes' to your project or to say, 'Yes, I'll do this. Yes,' you know? And then suddenly everybody says yes. Suddenly everybody wants you to do everything and anything you want."

The incredible success of *American Graffiti* could easily have sent George down this path. But he was able to resist temptation, in part because of his solid upbringing and his marriage to Marcia. But more than anything, it was George's passion for movies—and one movie in particular—that kept his feet on the ground.

Even though *THX 1138* had bombed at the box office, George still believed that there was a place for science fiction in American cinema. At the same time, he was interested in creating a modern myth that dealt with the forces of good and evil. These two ideas were the beginning of a movie called *Star Wars.*

With the proceeds from *American Graffiti*, George bought a Victorian home in Marin County, California, that would serve as the new headquarters for Lucasfilm Ltd., George's

newfound film company. It was here that *Star Wars* was finally born.

For eight hours a day, five days a week, George locked himself in a back room of the old house and worked on the script. As research, he studied other science-fiction and fantasy stories, as well as some of his old favorite comic books, including *Flash Gordon*. George also researched world religions, from Buddhism to Christianity. And he studied the American

anthropologist Joseph Campbell, who wrote extensively about mythology.

As George wrote and rewrote, the notion of the "Force" came into sharper focus. In the screenplay, the character of Obi-Wan Kenobi defines it as "an energy field created by all living things. It surrounds us and penetrates us; it binds the galaxy together."

The Force can be used for good or evil. This tension was central to what George was trying to create with *Star Wars*. As he later explained, "I wanted to make a kids' film that would strengthen contemporary mythology and introduce a basic kind of morality. Nobody's saying the very basic things. They're dealing in the abstract. Everybody's forgetting to tell the kids, 'Hey, this is right and this is wrong.' "

In order to get those pretty heavy ideas across, George knew that his story had to be fairly simple. In May 1974, after a year of work, he finally finished the first draft. It was close, but nowhere near finished. After another year of sweat and tears (and countless sheets of paper and No. 2 hard pencils), he had a more finished script that he was ready to shop around.

George knew that the world he'd created was so **fantastical** that the studio executives would have a hard time getting it. So he hired a commercial illustrator named Ralph McQuarrie to create paintings to bring his vision to life.

Film Notes
Star Wars (1977)

George's job: Writer and Director

What's it about?

This is the story of Luke Skywalker, a simple farm boy, who is called on to help rebel forces rescue Princess Leia from the clutches of Darth Vader and the evil Empire. Luke is joined by a team of allies that includes Han Solo, Chewbacca the Wookiee, and robotic sidekicks, C-3PO and R2-D2. *Star Wars* is actually Episode IV in Lucas's epic series, though it was the first one made. In the climactic final scene, Luke leads the rebels in an attack on the Empire's most dangerous weapon, the Death Star.

Main stars:

Mark Hamill as Luke Skywalker

Carrie Fisher as Princess Leia Organa

Harrison Ford as Han Solo

Alec Guinness as Ben "Obi-Wan" Kenobi

James Earl Jones as the voice of Darth Vader

Even with the paintings and George's success from *American Graffiti*, many studios still passed on the project. But Twentieth Century Fox saw the film's potential and gave it the green light. By this time, George realized that his script was too big for one movie, so he divided it into three parts. He wanted to make sure he'd keep control of all three parts. So he settled for an extremely low director's fee—$150,000 instead of the $500,000 he easily could have demanded—in exchange for the sequel and merchandising rights. The studio executives must have thought George was crazy, but this is now considered one of the boldest moves in Hollywood history.

With a deal in hand, it was time to cast the movie. As with *American Graffiti*, George insisted on fresh faces. He chose Mark Hamill, a relatively unknown TV actor, for the part of Luke Skywalker. Carrie Fisher, who had

trained in England as an actor, landed the role of Princess Leia. Harrison Ford, who had a small part in *American Graffiti*, would play Han Solo. To satisfy the studio executives, who always want big-name stars in every role, George picked the successful English star Alec Guinness to play Ben "Obi-Wan" Kenobi.

Next, George and his team scouted locations, which was challenging since the action takes place in outer space. A desert in Tunisia was perfect for the openings scenes set on the desert planet of Tatooine. But George realized that he would have to rely on computer-generated special effects for much of the other scenes. This was a fairly new field at the time, so George decided to open his own special effects studio in California called Industrial Light & Magic (ILM).

George brought in the best and brightest young people he could find to create the nearly

Danger on the Set!

Even with George's tight control of the production of *Star Wars*, mishaps were inevitable. During the desert shots, for example, a sandstorm kept knocking over the sets and caused R2-D2's electronic controls to fail. In another scene, one of the stormtroopers suffered a concussion and had to be sent to the hospital. Amid the challenges, George wrote to Marcia back home, "I forget how impossible making movies really is. I get so depressed, but I guess I'll get through it somehow."

three hundred and sixty special effects used in *Star Wars*. There were technical whizzes who knew who how to operate computer-controlled cameras; artists who designed the various costumes and spacecrafts, including the **iconic** Death Star; and sound engineers who could come up with the perfect sound track.

After a seemingly never-ending editing session, in which George and Marcia masterfully pieced together the special effects and film footage, *Star Wars* was finally ready for the big screen. There were some bigwigs in Hollywood who still thought the film would flop. Even George was nervous. But any doubts would soon be silenced forever.

Star Wars opened on forty-three screens across the country on May 25, 1977. As word spread, the movie opened in hundreds more theaters before taking the country, and then the entire world, by storm. It would go on to be one of the most successful movies of all time, earning ten Academy Awards nominations and earning $775 million worldwide. George certainly celebrated this success. But not for long. After all, there were still two more installments of the *Star Wars* trilogy to make.

CHAPTER
SEVEN

The Challenge of the Sequel

There's a reason the studio executives at Twentieth Century Fox were quick to surrender sequel rights to George during the negotiations of *Star Wars*. At the time, there really hadn't been many sequels that became box-office hits.

George was ready to prove the execs wrong with his second installment of the *Star Wars* trilogy. But first, he would end up proving them very right with a sequel to *American Graffiti.*

The truth is, George really wasn't that interested in the project, but Universal Studios wanted to cash in on the success of the first film, not to mention George's sudden stardom as the creator of *Star Wars*.

George decided not to direct *More American Graffiti*, but he would maintain control as executive producer. The story followed the same characters from the original, but it explored deeper, darker themes, including the devastation of the Vietnam War. Unfortunately, audiences found the film depressing, and the 1979 sequel was a flop.

More American Graffiti hardly served as a confidence booster as George turned his attention to *The Empire Strikes Back*. As the title suggested, part two of the original *Star Wars* trilogy would give the upper hand to the "Dark Side" in the epic battle between good and evil. Would audiences again be let down?

George admits, "I was nervous when I started the second film."

George spent several months working on a first draft for the movie. He knew it needed work, so he brought in another writer to revise the story. Meanwhile, George worked on reassembling his creative team from the original movie. Given the success of *Star Wars*, most everyone was thrilled to return.

George also had no trouble luring back the cast members. After all, *Star Wars* had made household names out of Mark Hamill, Carrie Fisher, and Harrison Ford, among others. There were some new roles to fill, most notably the character of Lando Calrissian. One of the few criticisms of *Star Wars* was that it didn't have enough minority actors. So George decided to go with Billy Dee Williams, an African American actor whose performance in *Lady Sings the Blues* he admired.

Creating Yoda

One of the biggest challenges of *The Empire Strikes Back* was creating Yoda, the two-foot-tall swamp creature who trains Luke Skywalker in the ways of the Jedi Knights. George's special-effects team created a puppet for Yoda, and his scenes were enhanced with the use of computer animation. Frank Oz, one of the first Muppet performers, performed and provided the voice of Yoda.

George felt good about the cast and crew, though he wouldn't be the one calling the shots on set. That's because George had made the difficult decision to not direct *The Empire Strikes Back*. "As a director, I wanted to do everything," he explained. "It's very hard for

Film Notes
The Empire Strikes Back (1980)

George's job: Executive producer and Co-writer

What's it about?

Episode V of the series picks
up where *Star Wars* left
off. Though the rebel forces
destroyed the Death Star, the
evil Empire is far from finished.
Under Darth Vader's evil
command, Imperial troops wage
a devastating attack on the icy
tundra of the planet Hoth that

ends with the capture of Han Solo, Chewbacca, and
Princess Leia. Meanwhile, Luke Skywalker follows
Obi-Wan Kenobi's command and journeys to the
swamp world of Dagobah to receive Jedi training
from Master Yoda. The movie ends with a startling
discovery by Luke about Darth Vader's true identity.

Main stars:

Mark Hamill as Luke Skywalker

Carrie Fisher as Princess Leia Organa

Harrison Ford as Han Solo

Billy Dee Williams as Lando Calrissian

Frank Oz as the voice of Yoda

me to delegate things to other people. Well, the best way to do that is to take one more step back and be forced to delegate everything. And see if I could stand it."

George turned the directing reigns over to a veteran Hollywood director named Irvin Kershner. At first, the two men clashed due to their conflicting styles—George liked a fast pace while Irvin preferred to spend time with each scene—but they eventually made it work. And George was very much in control of the film's editing and special effects, so much so that he was just as exhausted by *The Empire Strikes Back* as he was by *Star Wars*. He also spent about $33 million of his own money trying to get the movie just right.

Even with George's significant influence on *The Empire Strikes Back*, he still wondered whether audiences would embrace it. But from the moment it opened on May 21, 1980, it

was clear that the sequel to *Star Wars* would be every bit as popular as the original. In its first weekend alone, the movie made almost $5 million. That's nothing compared to the more than $530 million it would eventually earn worldwide.

Obviously, fans weren't bothered by the dark story line of *The Empire Strikes Back*. Maybe that's because they knew there was still more to come in the story. And they couldn't wait to see where George would take them.

CHAPTER EIGHT

A Guy Named Indy

Moviegoers worldwide were desperate to learn how the *Star Wars* trilogy would end. But first they would be introduced to another of the greatest characters in all of cinema: Indiana Jones.

The story of the adventurous **archaeology** professor had been bouncing around in George's head for many years. He'd taken some archaeology classes at Modesto Junior College, so the seed for the story may have been planted then. In 1975, he discussed the idea with the director and screenwriter Philip Kaufman, who suggested he incorporate the Ark of the Covenant into the story. In the Bible, the covenant is a lost chest that contains the stone tablets with the Ten Commandments on them. George filed the story away while he worked on *Star Wars*.

George made a habit of taking a relaxing beach vacation during the premiere of his films, "so I miss all the craziness that goes on, all the hoopla, and the hype and the success, and how much it's making, or whether it's doing good or whether it's doing bad."

When *Star Wars* opened in 1977, he chose Hawaii as his great escape. And he invited his friend Steven Spielberg to come along. Among the topics the two men discussed was George's idea for a film called *Raiders of the Lost Ark*.

He wanted Spielberg to be the director.

It's difficult to imagine a more talented creative team working on a movie. Spielberg had directed two of the biggest films of the 1970s, *Jaws* and *Close Encounters of the Third Kind*, and he would go on to make many more, from *E.T.* to *Jurassic Park*.

The question was: Could two men with such strong creative visions learn to **collaborate**? At first, it didn't look likely. George wanted

the film to be like the cliff-hanger TV shows he used to watch as a kid, while Spielberg preferred nonstop thrills. As for the character, George wanted Indiana to be a maverick, but ultimately a good guy, kind of like Han Solo. Spielberg saw him as more of a rebel.

The two power players also disagreed over the casting of Indiana Jones. Like always, George wanted to come up with a relative unknown. He was interested in Tom Selleck, who was about to start work on the TV series *Magnum, P.I.* When they couldn't get him, Spielberg suggested Harrison Ford. George resisted at first, but finally agreed.   .

It turned out to be the right decision. Ford was perfect for the part, bringing the right blend of confidence, humor, and **humility**. George and Steven learned to work through their creative differences, and the film was actually shot in just seventy-three days, finishing two weeks

Film Notes
Raiders of the Lost Ark (1981)

George's job: Executive producer and Co-writer

What's it about?

Set in the 1930s, this is the story of renowned archaeology professor Dr. Indiana Jones, who is hired by the U.S. government to find the Ark of the Covenant, thought to be somewhere near the city of Cairo, in Egypt. The Ark is believed to carry great power, which the government does not want to fall into the hands of the evil Nazis. The Nazis have hired their own archaeologist, Indiana's longtime rival Rene Belloq, to rescue the ark. That sets up a classic contest between good and evil and a nonstop series of battles and adventures.

Main stars:

Harrison Ford as Indiana Jones

Paul Freeman as René Belloq

Karen Allen as Marion Ravenwood

John Rhys-Davies as Sallah

ahead of schedule. George then got to work with editor Michael Kahn to tighten up the story and establish the perfect pace.

Raiders of the Lost Ark opened on June 14, 1981. In its first weekend alone, it earned more than $8 million. It would go on to rake in nearly $400 million. And *Raiders* was just the beginning. In 1984, the world's most-loved archaeologist returned in *Indiana Jones and the Temple of Doom*, with George producing

and Spielberg directing. It did nearly as well, earning more than $330 million worldwide. More movies would follow, as well as several TV spinoffs.

George couldn't have had many doubters after *Star Wars*. But with the success of the Indiana Jones saga, his place in history as one of the greatest Hollywood legends was secure.

CHAPTER
NINE

Back to the Empire

With the success of *Raiders of the Lost Ark*, George was clearly on a roll. But in the cutthroat world of Hollywood, you're only as good as your last film. Plus, he knew if the final installment of the *Star Wars* trilogy flopped, fans would never forget it. And so, as George started in on the project, he was definitely feeling the heat.

In times of pressure, George must have thought it best to go with what worked in the past. That was very much George's strategy with *Return of the Jedi*. As with *Empire Strikes Back*, George would serve as executive producer. He brought in Lawrence Kasdan, a writer on *Empire Strikes Back*, to help him with the screenplay. He hired Richard Marquand to direct, though George would be on set every day. And the cast of actors remained the same.

As with the first two *Star Wars* episodes, special effects were a major part of the production. George took advantage of the latest technologies. For example, the speederbike scenes on the forest moon, Endor, were filmed with the Steadicam, a stabilized camera that's worn on a harness by the cameraperson. Some scenes were shot in California's Redwood National Park, with the actors later added in with computers.

Then there were the Ewoks, teddy bear–like creatures who lived in the towering trees.

Film Notes
Return of the Jedi (1983)

George's job: Executive producer and Co-writer

What's it about?

Episode VI of the series opens with the building of a new Death Star by Darth Vader and the Galactic Empire. Meanwhile, Luke Skywalker and Princess Leia rescue Han Solo from the evil gangster Jabba the Hutt. Luke then returns to Master Yoda to complete his Jedi training, and learns more about his relationship with Darth Vader, as well as his connection to Princess Leia. Luke returns to destroy the Death Star, where he engages in a final battle between good and evil with Darth Vader. The force of good prevails, and the rebels go on to destroy the Death Star and defeat the evil Empire once and for all.

Main stars:

Mark Hamill as Luke Skywalker

Carrie Fisher as Princess Leia Organa

Harrison Ford as Han Solo

Peter Mayhew as Chewbacca the Wookiee

Ian McDiarmid as the Emperor

Though audience members might have thought the Ewoks were computer generated, they were actually played by little people dressed in elaborate costumes. Fans were also introduced to Jabba the Hutt, the gangster-like creature who is talked about, but never seen, in the original *Star Wars*.

Return of the Jedi opened on May 25, 1983, six years to the day after the release of the

original. Fans were beside themselves with anticipation, so much so that no one really doubted that the film would be a hit. And a hit it was. In its opening weekend alone, *Return of the Jedi* nearly made its money back, earning about $30 million. It would go on to make more than $475 million worldwide.

George had given his audience the ending they craved. But by then they were well aware of the fact that *Return of the Jedi* concluded the *second* trilogy of the *Star Wars* epic. That meant there was more to come. But when?

To the disappointment of die-hard *Star Wars* fans, the answer to that question was about fifteen years later. George had been consumed by *Star Wars* for the better part of the last decade, so it's understandable that he wanted a break. He focused on other projects, some successful, like the various Indiana Jones movies and spinoffs, and some not so successful, like *Howard the Duck*.

But through it all, he never stopped thinking about *Star Wars*. Ever the perfectionist, he even continued to think about the films that had already been made. As the twentieth anniversary of the original *Star Wars* approached, he decided he would rerelease all three movies. Besides restoring the films, which had deteriorated, he also shot new scenes and even added back scenes that had been cut from the original films, using the latest technologies. For example, he was able to show Jabba the Hutt in the original film, as he'd originally intended. *Star Wars* had been "about forty percent of what I wanted it to be," he had said.

The rereleases were nearly as big as the original releases, and brought in a whole new generation of fans. All three films premiered in the number one spot and earned hundreds of millions of dollars in profits. It was just the momentum booster George needed to start in on the first trilogy of the *Star Wars* series.

CHAPTER
TEN

Back to the
Beginning

The second *Star Wars* trilogy had a built-in audience: millions of fans who had seen the original. And the rerelease of the early films had attracted a whole new generation of fans. In that sense, the second trilogy was pretty much a guaranteed success. But at the same time, George was under a lot of pressure to create a trilogy that lived up to the *Star Wars* standard.

Once again, George went with what had

worked for him in the past. That meant continuing the story line of good versus evil. The first trilogy is primarily about how Anakin Skywalker, father of Luke Skywalker, became Darth Vader. "He was a sweet kid, helpful, just like most people imagine themselves to be," George said. "He eventually realizes he's going down the dark path, but he thinks it's justifiable. The idea is to see how a **democracy** becomes a **dictatorship**, and how a good person goes bad—and still, in the end, thinks he's doing the right thing."

In this sense, the first story is basically the backstory to the second trilogy that fans already knew so well (it's often referred to as the *Star Wars* "prequel trilogy"). Given that twenty years had passed, George couldn't use any of the same actors. There was great anticipation over who would form the cast of the new movies. Fans were especially excited to see

who would be the young Obi-Wan Kenobi, played by Alec Guinness in the original. The role went to Ewan McGregor, a respected and popular Scottish actor.

To play the grown Anakin Skywalker, who doesn't show up until Episode II, George chose Canadian actor Hayden Christensen. Hayden was relatively unknown at the time, but George liked him because he had good on-screen chemistry with Natalie Portman, who played the part of Padmé, Luke and Leia's mother.

From Film to Digital

Star Wars: Episode II - Attack of the Clones was one of the first major films to be shot almost entirely with high-definition digital cameras, rather than with conventional film. Some traditionalists criticized the decision, arguing that digital cameras change the look of movies. But the technology is now widely used in Hollywood, another example of George's vision and pioneering spirit.

After not directing the last two films of the original *Star Wars* trilogy, George decided to direct the entire first trilogy. The move surprised some in Hollywood, who thought George had left the director's chair for good. But for George, the temptation of bringing new technologies to the *Star Wars* epic was too great.

The experience of finally being able to bring Jabba the Hutt to life during the rerelease of

Star Wars showed him the possibilities. "I could do other things that up to that point had been impossible," he says. "The success of that rerelease not only told me that I could create these creatures and build better sets and towns than I could before, but that the *Star Wars* audience was still alive—it hadn't completely disappeared after fifteen years."

Indeed, it hadn't. When *Star Wars: Episode I - The Phantom Menace* finally opened on May 19, 1999, the legion of *Star Wars* fans could

Film Notes
The Phantom Menace (1999)

George's job: Executive producer, Writer, and Director

What's it about?

The first movie in the *Star Wars* series features a young Obi-Wan Kenobi and his mentor and fellow Jedi Knight, Qui-Gon Jinn. The duo embark on an adventure to save the peace-loving planet Naboo from the evil Trade Federation. They are joined by Queen Amidala and a Gungan outcast named Jar Jar Binks. Later, they enlist the help of a young and gifted slave child named Anakin Skywalker.

Main stars:

Ewan McGregor as Obi-Wan Kenobi

Natalie Portman as Padmé Amidala

Liam Neeson as Qui-Gon Jinn

Jake Lloyd as Young Anakin Skywalker

hardly contain themselves. The movie made more than $64 million on its opening weekend, and would go on to earn more than $1 billion worldwide. *Episode II - Attack of the Clones*, which opened on May 16, 2002, took in about $650 million worldwide. And the grand finale, *Episode III - Revenge of the Sith*, added just under $850 million.

Even Hollywood legends have their critics, and so there were those who doubted George's ability to succeed with the *Star Wars* prequel trilogy. But as the films' incredible profit and popularity showed, the Force was still very much with George. The only question left was: How would he use it next?

Life After
Star Wars

In a January 2012 interview with the *New York Times*, George uttered the two words his fans have feared most: "I'm retiring." At the age of sixty-seven, he felt he had accomplished all he could possibly accomplish as a creator of blockbuster films.

Rumors swirled for years about a third *Star Wars* trilogy. But George insisted they were nothing more than rumors. "I get asked all the time, 'What happens after *Return of the*

Jedi?' and there really is no answer for that," he said. "The movies were the story of Anakin Skywalker and Luke Skywalker, and when Luke saves the galaxy and redeems his father, that's where that story ends."

Despite all of George's denials, it seems there *is* still a *Star Wars* story to tell. In 2012, after Lucasfilm Ltd. was acquired by the Walt Disney Company for over $4 billion, it was announced that new *Star Wars* films will be made. George will have to wait a little longer to retire, as he will serve as the creative consultant for the movies.

There's another reason George could never leave films completely: The industry has literally grown up around him. Lucasfilm, the production company he founded in 1971, is one of the industry's most successful operations, which helps explain why Disney was willing to pay so much to own it. The Lucasfilm paycheck did not go to George, however, as he instead decided to donate almost all of it to charity.

Lucasfilm was originally headquartered at Skywalker Ranch in Northern California, which George bought in 1978 with proceeds from *American Graffiti*. George was heavily involved in the design of the ranch, which he saw as a kind of creative laboratory for filmmaking, along the lines of what he knew from his film-school days.

Lucasfilm Ltd. has expanded beyond Skywalker Ranch to four campuses worldwide. It includes several divisions. There's Industrial Light & Magic (ILM), the special-effects company created for the first *Star Wars* film that is now one of most successful of its kind, having contributed to such films as *Jurassic Park* and *Avatar*.

Skywalker Sound is another division of the company devoted to sound design and audio post-production, aspects of filmmaking that George has always valued highly. He once even said, "Sound is fifty percent of the motion picture experience."

One of the busiest divisions of Lucasfilm is Lucas Licensing, which handles the merchandising relating to *Star Wars*, Indiana Jones, and other properties. All the T-shirts,  books, posters, action figures, and more that have been sold over the years in more than one hundred countries have added up to more than $20 billion in sales.

That's allowed George to also follow many philanthropic pursuits. For example, in 1991, he founded Lucas Learning, which looks for ways to use technology to promote education. "Many years ago as a filmmaker I developed an interest in interactive technologies," George said. "As I began to work in this area, I realized the great potential for opening up new kinds of learning experiences for young people."

In addition to raising three children of his own, this effort to help others has become George's focus. "You can find people rich, powerful, and famous, and they aren't happy," George said. "And you can find people who have discovered the fact that it's really helping people, it's really being **compassionate** toward other human beings that makes you happy, that gives you a spiritual fulfillment—a kind of fulfillment that goes way beyond anything you can buy."

10 Things

You Should Know
About George Lucas

1 George was born on May 14, 1944. George has two older sisters and one younger sister.

2 George's original dream in life was to become a race-car driver, but that changed when he got into a terrible car accident as a teenager.

George was part of a new group of directors from the 1970s who learned their craft at film school. He and his peers are sometimes referred to as the Film School Generation.

 George was diagnosed with diabetes in his twenties. The discovery kept him from being drafted into the Vietnam War.

 In order to bring his vision of *Star Wars* to life, George started his own special—effects company called Industrial Light & Magic, which helped transform Hollywood.

6 George is extremely interested in mythology. *Star Wars* was influenced

by the teachings of Joseph Campbell, who wrote the book *The Hero with a Thousand Faces*.

7 Though George has directed some of the most successful films of all time, he actually prefers the editing side of filmmaking.

8 George's decision to secure the merchandising and sequel rights to *Star Wars* in exchange for a lower director's fee is one of the most profitable gambles in the history of Hollywood.

Along with Lucas Learning, George founded the George Lucas Educational Foundation, which publishes Edutopia, a website dedicated to transforming the learning process through technology, teacher development, and other strategies.

 George has three children, all of whom are adopted.

10 MORE Things

That Are Pretty Cool to Know

1 Even though George is a billionaire, with a net worth of more than $7 billion, he almost always wears the same outfit, which consists of a flannel shirt, blue jeans, and beat—up sneakers.

2 Indiana Jones was named after George's dog, Indiana. But he originally called the character Indiana Smith. Steven Spielberg convinced him to change it to Indiana Jones.

3 George wrote the entire *Star Wars* screenplay on paper with a No. 2 pencil.

4 *Star Wars* was originally imagined as one movie, but George realized the story was too big, so he divided it into three parts.

5 Skywalker Ranch is located on Lucas Valley Road, though the name of the road is pure coincidence.

6 George's nickname in high school was Luke.

7 George was initially interested in Tom Selleck for the part of Indiana Jones, but he eventually agreed to give it to Harrison Ford.

8 To come up with the sound of Chewbacca's voice, Ben Burtt and the sound engineers on *Star Wars* used a mix of bears, walruses, dogs, and lions.

 9 George always goes on a beach vacation during his films' premieres so that he misses all the hoopla.

10 *Star Wars: Episode I – The Phantom Menace* has earned more than $1 billion worldwide, making it the most successful of all the *Star Wars* films.

Glossary

Archaeology: the study of the distant past, which often involves digging up old buildings, objects, and bones and examining them carefully

Avid: very committed

Boundless: unlimited

Collaborate: to work together to do something

Compassionate: feeling sympathy for and a desire to help someone who is suffering

Corrupt: immoral

Democracy: a form of government in which the people choose their leaders in elections

Dictatorship: a form of government in which a ruler has complete control over the country

Fantastical: based on fantasy

Glamorize: to make something seem glamorous

Humility: the quality or state of being humble or modest

Iconic: very famous and well-known

Kindred: similar in kind

Perseverance: the quality of continuing to do something even if there are difficulties

Resemblance: the physical similarity between people or things

Studious: liking or tending to study very hard

Places to Visit

Want to learn more about George? There are plenty of places to visit, both online and in the real world. Here are a few to consider:

Modesto, California
George's hometown, located about ninety miles east of San Francisco.
ci.modesto.ca.us

Internet Movie Database
Short for "Internet Movie Database," IMDb.com is considered the number one movie website in the world.
IMDb.com

Lucasfilm Ltd.
The official website of George's production company.
Lucasfilm.com

Letterman Digital Arts Center
The San Francisco campus of Lucasfilm Ltd.
onelettermandrive.com

Bibliography

The Cinema of George Lucas, Marcus Hearn, Harry N. Abrams, 2005.

George Lucas: Creator of Star Wars, Dana Meachen Rau and Christopher Rau, Franklin Watts, 1999.

George Lucas: Interviews, Edited by Sally Kline, University Press of Mississippi, 1999.

Mythmaker: The Life and Work of George Lucas, John Baxter, Avon Books, 1999.

Skywalking and the Films of George Lucas, Dale Pollock, Harmony Books, 1993

Ten American Movie Directors: The Men Behind the Camera, Anne E. Hill, Enslow Publishers, 2003.

Index

Also Available